Lizzie McGuire

life with lizzie

A Journal by Lizzie and Me!

SCHOLASTIC INC.
New York Toronto London Auckland Sydney
Mexico City New Delhi Hong Kong Buenos Aires

Welcome to Day One of your brand-new life.

You're on the brink of being the best of all possible things – as cool as the cutest girl in school, as smart as the biggest brainiac you know, and as happy as any sane person is on the first day of summer vacation.

Why, you ask?

BECAUSE YOU'RE ABOUT TO GET ORGANIZED!

This year, you and I are going to get our lives under control – whatever it takes. Just follow my lead, and we'll conquer the chaos of life, including all those obnoxious cheerleaders, ridiculous popular kids, disgusting science projects, and unanswerable math problems.

Here's your chance to brush off the hard knocks, tough breaks, and geeky accessories of the last 12 months and say, "Excuse me! But in case you haven't noticed – I'm cool now!" And you will be – cool, calm, and collected.

Along the way, I'll keep you posted on all the crucial info you'll need as you walk the road to total popularity (while maintaining a true and meaningful inner sense of yourself, of course). I would never want to encourage outrageous popularity at the risk of becoming a shallow and nasty she-devil – not much, anyway.

So, use your journal, stay organized, shop often, and never say no to junk food. We'll get through this year one month at a time.

Lizzie

Just tell me where I'm supposed to be and when I'm supposed to be there and I'll take care of the rest....

the workaday weekdays, aka the basic schedj ...
semester one

	MONDAY	TUESDAY	WEDNESDAY	THURSDAY	FRIDAY
1ST PERIOD					
2ND PERIOD					
3RD PERIOD					
4TH PERIOD					
5TH PERIOD					
6TH PERIOD					
7TH PERIOD					
8TH PERIOD					
AFTER SCHOOL!					

A NEW SEMESTER!!!
Nothing like a little
change of pace to
brighten up your day.

the workaday weekdays,
aka the basic schedj . . .

semester two

	MONDAY	TUESDAY	WEDNESDAY	THURSDAY	FRIDAY
1ST PERIOD					
2ND PERIOD					
3RD PERIOD					
4TH PERIOD					
5TH PERIOD					
6TH PERIOD					
7TH PERIOD					
8TH PERIOD					
AFTER SCHOOL!					

step 1: surviving school

So, in the old days – back before I became an Organizational Superhero – I couldn't get further than my class schedule before I was on a major overload, full-frontal freak-out! I'd go running from school screaming, "How am I supposed to do all the work for these classes PLUS put in the necessary time on after-school projects in order to have lots of friends and be a normal well-adjusted kid with happy childhood memories when I'm an adult?"

Okay – so I didn't actually run screaming from school. Instead, I took a deep breath, closed my eyes, and reminded myself that this was just the beginning. Anything new is overwhelming until you get used to it. The best thing to do is write it all down.

So that's my plan. I'll just write it all down, every last assignment, due date, and test day, my monthly goals, and important dates like birthdays, holidays, and anniversaries. I'll keep all the phone numbers I might need alphabetized and neatly written. I'll keep a daily list of everything I need to bring home in order to get the work done. (Uh-oh – how am I ever going to keep track of all the things I need to keep track of? I'll have to make a list. But then that's something else I need to keep track of! Okay, breathe. Breathe. I can do this. Right?)

I'm so all over this! I just need to set up the system and then – I'll be golden!

month _November_

The subjects in school that I don't completely hate (okay, I admit it, I even like a couple of them) are:

1. Math
2. SIR time
3. DEAR Time
4.
5.

The subjects that I could totally do without:

1. Math
2. Recess
3. Lunch
4.
5.

And so it begins... sigh.

SO BORED
BY THE
FIRE. CHILLIN.
WRITING
IN A JOURNA

monday

tuesday

wednesday

thursday

friday

sat./sun.

Week number two and I'm still alive.... How about you?

month _____

monday

tuesday

wednesday

thursday

friday

sat./sun.

Three weeks of organizing and I'm ready for a break – or at least a field trip. Here's where I'd go:

1. The mall
2. Paris
3. Tahiti (the beach can be very educational)
4. Uh . . . the mall

How about you?

1. Mall
2. Spa
3. friend house

4. Beach

Note to self – breathe.

BORED

Have you said hello to someone you don't know this month? No time like the present!

month _____

monday

tuesday

wednesday

thursday

friday

sat./sun.

Your thoughts on the month? Jot down a few notes. . . .

_____
_____
_____
_____
_____
_____
_____
_____
_____
_____
_____
_____
_____
_____
_____
_____
_____
_____
_____
_____

Where does the time go?

interspecies diplomacy
(or: getting along with cheerleaders)

Repeat after me: Football is the root of all evil. Why, you ask? Why am I picking on a bunch of guys who've been head-butted too many times to be sure of their first names?

Because if it weren't for football, there wouldn't be cheerleaders and if there weren't cheer-leaders, I would be a much happier person. If football is the root of all evil, then cheerleaders are the fully blossomed stink flower on the top of the plant that grows from that root.

I'm sorry. Do I sound bitter? Well, there's a reason for that. I AM! There I was, minding my own well-organized business in social studies, when I suddenly hear my name and then (head cheer-leader/ex-friend) Kate's name and then the word *partners*.

Huh?! I have to be partners with Kate on a project called The Importance of Diplomacy *and it will represent half my grade for the whole semester?* Stop! Help! This is not possible, not to mention just a wee bit UNJUST!

Deep breaths. I must stay calm. This too shall pass.

Basically, cheerleaders exist. It's a fact. You gotta figure out how to live with 'em because it's not likely they'll fall off the top of the human pyramid every time you wish they would.

The key to diplomacy Lizzie-style is "know thyself"! If you feel confident about who you are and how you handle things, it'll be harder for someone else to shake you up. (Okay. No one is allowed to mention the word *Kate*.) Time for a little personality quiz.

Answer yes or no to the following questions:

1. You've been given the heinous job of team captain in gym class. You know the new kid has two left legs but you pick him anyway because winning is not everything. No

2. The boy you like hangs with a group that's bullying the geeks. You approach heartthrob-dude and say, "I suspect you could be a better human being if you tried." No

3. Your little brother answers the phone by saying, "Did you know my sister sleeps in footie pajamas with bunny ears?" You playfully nudge your brother and remind him that there are better ways to get attention. No

Another month, another chance at perfection . . .

monday

tuesday

wednesday

thursday

I'm okay.
You're okay.
OKAY?!
Whatever!

friday

sat./sun.

month _____

monday

tuesday

wednesday

thursday

friday

sat./sun.

You guessed it – more questions. Yes or no:

4. You happen to be really popular so you're nominated for student government president along with a kid who'd be really good but is a total doofus. You decline the nomination and give a speech about tolerance and inner beauty.

5. You got the last mini pizza from the vending machine and the football player behind you sighs with great disappointment. You put aside your bitterness toward his sport and give him half the pizza.

Count up the number of times you answered YES to a question:

1-2: It might not be a bad idea to brush up on your people skills. Start with a smile.

3-4: You make friends easily but you could be a little nicer to the kid who needs a friend.

5: You should be an international diplomat.

It's lunchtime. Do you know where your friends are?

monday

tuesday

wednesday

thursday

friday

sat./sun.

month _____

monday

tuesday

wednesday

thursday

friday

sat./sun.

Don't forget to make a few notes on life this month. . . .

Another month, another meltdown . . .

listen up! communicate!

The highly evolved Anti-Chaos Superhero knows that communication is at the center of all things Organized.

Whether you're talking to your friends, your enemies (such as a cheerleader), or your teachers, you must keep the information flowing! Sometimes you might discover that the best way to communicate is with yourself.

Example: Kate usually just stares blankly at me when I speak. So I've found it's far more effective to talk to myself in order to keep things on course with our "joint" project.

Anyway, when speaking to myself, I do it out loud so that Kate at least hears the words – even if she doesn't understand them. Perhaps she will bring them back to her spaceship and others from her planet can decode them.

FYI: The diplomacy assignment is to explore a current tension-filled situation anywhere in the world and show how diplomacy could be used to resolve the conflict. Hmmmm. What should I pick? Oh! I know! How about . . . my life!

month _____

monday

tuesday

wednesday

thursday

friday

sat./sun.

The right vocabulary is totally key to communication. Words can so make or break a diplomatic effort. Let me put it to you this way – there are people out there who actually think the right words are more important than the right shoes! So – pay attention!

1. CONE OF SILENCE: a deadly serious vow between friends to say nothing about a certain person, place, and/or thing.

2. SHE-GEEK: a way not-cool girl.

3. HEL-LO-O?: an expression of amazement used when someone misses the very obvious.

If you can't say something nice – say something funny!

monday

tuesday

wednesday

thursday

friday

sat./sun.

Floccinaucinihilipilification

I don't know if it's the right word but it's the longest one in the English dictionary.

(FYI: It means "the action of estimating as worthless." Oka-a-ay. Whatever.)

monday

Pop quiz! Did you pay attention? Then you should be able to fill in the blanks.

Even though Miranda vowed the _____ , she accidentally told the whole school that I called Kate a _sheqeek_ because even though she's totally cool, she's totally not, if you know what I mean. _____ , Miranda. Did that really need to be repeated?

tuesday

wednesday

thursday

Say what?

friday

sat./sun.

More awesome vocab:

monday

tuesday

wednesday

thursday

Greetings and salutations!

Don't you just love big words?

friday

sat./sun.

month _____

monday

tuesday

wednesday

thursday

friday

sat./sun.

Another month bites the dust . . . jot down a few notes about it. . . .

Heads up!
Fresh month ahead!

shopping is <u>not</u> for the unorganized!

And so we come to one of the best and most important reasons to be organized—shopping.

Organizing your life will benefit your shopping skills in the following ways:

1. You gain a better sense of exactly how much time you can spend at the mall.

2. You know precisely how much money you can spend.

3. You are aware of every last birthday, holiday, and special event so that you've always got the totally perfect explanation for your mother as to exactly why you must go shopping right now, today, this instant! No ifs, ands, or buts!

When it comes to shopping and organization, I have one word of advice: LISTS! They are the who, what, where, when, and why of shopping. Don't leave home without them – make 'em, follow 'em, love 'em!

monday

List #1: I will earn shopping money by doing the following jobs:
1. Mowing Lawns
2. Singing to Children
3.
4.
5.

tuesday

List #2: I want to find the perfect gift for the following people:

PERSON	GIFT IDEA
1.	
2.	
3.	
4.	
5.	

wednesday

thursday

Buyer **beware!**

Shopping is not for amateurs.

friday

sat./sun.

monday

tuesday

wednesday

thursday

friday

'Tis better to **shop** than to receive.

sat./sun.

month _____

monday

tuesday

wednesday

thursday

friday

sat./sun.

List #3: Without sounding too materialistic, should someone ask, I would like the following gifts:
1.
2.
3.
4.
5.

List #4: In the true spirit of gift giving and receiving, these are the people and things I treasure the most:
1.
2.
3.
4.
5.

Only 365 **shopping days** left
– until next year at this time!

Never trust someone who doesn't like to **shop.**

monday

tuesday

wednesday

thursday

friday

sat./sun.

month _____

monday

tuesday

wednesday

thursday

friday

sat./sun.

Your thoughts on the month?

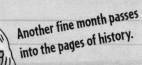

Another fine month passes into the pages of history.

fitness for couch potatoes

If you ask me, resolutions are overrated. Personally, I've never successfully resolved – resoluted – been resolutely – oh, you know what I mean! But since I've already made one resolution this year (remember that whole "get my life under control" thing?), I figured, what's one more?

Besides, when it comes to physical fitness, sometimes it takes a butt-kicking, muscle-ripping resolution to get you to do it. So wipe the slate clean and start fresh.

So . . .
I resolve to exercise and eat right . . . for at least one month before crumbling.

month _____

monday

tuesday

wednesday

thursday

friday

sat./sun.

Atten-hut! Shake it out! It's time to commit to a real regimen. Fill in the blanks and do it with a smile on your face!

1. I pledge I will exercise _____ times a week for _____ minutes a day. (Okay. Let's just say I'll try to exercise _____ times a week for _____ minutes a day.)

2. In order to improve my physical prowess (and release all those cool self-esteem endorphins), I will participate in the following activities so as to be exercised:
_____ , _____ and _____ .

3. When I exercise, I feel: _____
_____ .

My resolution is to **not** make any resolutions!

monday

tuesday

wednesday

thursday

Cowabunga!

friday

sat./sun.

month _____

monday

tuesday

wednesday

thursday

friday

sat./sun.

It's not always easy staying in shape and feeling fit. May I suggest the following activities to get you headed in the right direction:

1. When lying on the couch watching TV, don't just use your thumb on the remote control. Try using all your different fingers for a fine digital workout.

2. When talking on the phone with friends, pick one or two key words such as *like* or *Whatever!* Each time your friend says the chosen word, you must stand up and do a jumping jack.

3. When staring into the refrigerator in search of the perfect snack, do three deep knee bends for every item you select.

4. When going to the video rental store, choose a favorite actor or actress. Every time you see a movie with that person in it, you must jog up and down every aisle of the store.

I **would** exercise, but I fear I might become shallow if I get too **buff**.

monday

tuesday

wednesday

thursday

friday

sat./sun.

month _____

monday

tuesday

wednesday

thursday

friday

sat./sun.

How's your new fully fit self? Write down your thoughts. . . .

All right! Uncle! I'll admit it – I feel better when I exercise. Now go away!

unorganizable: l . . . l . . . l-ove

Ugh! Love loves chaos! You cannot file it away. You cannot cross it off the list. All you can do is proceed with caution!

You've seen it yourself: perfectly normal, sane American kids transform into gooey-eyed oglers. They'll go rubber-lipped at the sight of a person who three weeks ago they rightly thought was the lamest excuse for a human that existed.

People go nuts! Not that I'm against it, really – as long as there's someone staring gooey-eyed at me.

month _____

monday

tuesday

wednesday

thursday

friday

sat./sun.

TOP SECRET LIST:
If I had a crush (which, of course, I don't – hello!), I would have a crush on:

1.
2.
3.

TOP, TOP SECRET LIST:

It wouldn't be the *worst* thing in the world to get a love letter from:

1.
2.
3.

Warning!
Monday ahead!

DAD IS BORING

He loves me.

He loves me not.

He's responsible for me murdering this daisy!

monday

tuesday

wednesday

thursday

friday

sat./sun.

month _____

monday

tuesday

wednesday

thursday

friday

sat./sun.

So? Have you succumbed to the love bug? If so, you'll need a pet name for your boyfriend. Write down your possibilities here and, please, no "Snookums" or "Sweetpea" – I beg you!

1.
2.
3.
4.

And now I believe it's time to address that age-old question: What's the difference between a boyfriend and a friend that's a boy?

Okay. We've addressed it. And once again, I don't know the answer! But please, discuss it with your friends and get back to me!

Roses are red, violets are blue . . .
poems about love aren't usually true.

monday

tuesday

wednesday

thursday

friday

Is it **Friday** yet?

sat./sun.

month _____

monday

tuesday

wednesday

thursday

friday

sat./sun.

Your thoughts, please—jot down a few notes. . . .

Don't you find some weeks seem to go on for months?

s-t-r-e-t-c-h yourself!

Take a deep life-affirming breath.

Great. Feel better?

Okay. So maybe it takes a little more than a deep breath to break out of your routine. It's time to step back and take a good long look at what you're doing to expand your horizons.

Whatever that means! I mean, do you really want your horizon to expand? Isn't that potentially dangerous to the universe as a whole? If everybody goes around expanding their personal horizons, don't we run the risk of creating The Horizon That Ate Cleveland?!

All right – so let's just call it stretching yourself in new and interesting ways. Because the truth is, when you try something new you're bound to find out something about yourself you didn't know – not a bad thing.

For example, until my teacher informed me that I had to write a monster term paper on the giant tortoises of the Galápagos Islands, I had no idea how much I dislike reptiles. Not important? Ah, but it is. I can now narrow down my career choices to anything that doesn't involve scaly things. Good to know.

monday

tuesday

wednesday

thursday

friday

sat./sun.

What have you done this year in that vast realm known to the outside world as "extracurricular"? Drama Club? Spanish Club? A little Field Hockey? Not sure what you want to do? Make a list of three activities you enjoy doing.

1.
2.
3.

Now list three clubs or teams that match up with your "enjoyable activities" list:

1.
2.
3.

I enjoy finding things I don't particularly enjoy. Does that count?

monday

tuesday

wednesday

thursday

friday

sat./sun.

Nothing like a good **macramé** weaving session to set **me** straight!

month _____

monday

tuesday

wednesday

thursday

friday

sat./sun.

Now pick one of the organizations you listed on the last page and complete this pledge:

I _____ (your name) pledge that I will at least talk to someone about getting involved in _____ (the name of your organization). Following said discussion, I will then get involved. However, if after said discussion I decide the whole thing is totally lame (and not because I'm just nervous about trying something new), I have the option of finding something else.

_____   _____
(Sign your name here)   (today's date)

A brief moment of soul searching, please . . . How do you feel now that you've at least TRIED to try something new?

I feel . . .

Personally, gym is my best definition of "nightmare."

I feel . . . ready for a vacation!

month _____

monday

tuesday

wednesday

thursday

friday

sat./sun.

Ix-nay on this onth-may! How did it go for you? A few notes, please . . .

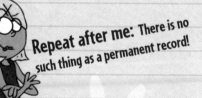

Repeat after me: There is no such thing as a permanent record!

you can't schedule the unexpected!

I schedule, I list, I plan, I plot—I could spontaneously combust under the weight of it all and still, I'm supposed to expect the unexpected?! Well, actually, that's way cool. Okay.

Here's my latest entry for the "Didn't Schedule That" file:

There I was, laminated to a chair in the library, buried in books about tortoises, and wondering what happened to my relatively enjoyable life. Suddenly, this guy I don't know is talking to me about giant tortoises. This guy LOVES these overgrown reptiles. He thinks they're as amazing as—oh, I don't know—say, finding the perfect hair accessory.

I'm not saying he's boyfriend material or anything, but Tortoise Guy did give me some great books. He also spent the entire afternoon spewing facts and figures about the ancient hard-backed beasts. And you know what? You're talking to an A student! (At least this week.)

So, three cheers for Tortoise Guy and four cheers for unscheduled surprises.

month _____

monday

tuesday

wednesday

thursday

friday

sat./sun.

Waiting for unscheduled surprises is like waiting for water to boil. In other words—get on with it! So where were we? Oh, right—on the road to being way cool and totally popular, in a non-shallow kind of way. Time to think about self-improvement. Do you want to break some bad habits or start some good ones? No time like the present. Name three habits you would like to break *or* develop.

1.
2.
3.

The most important part of wanting to change something is knowing why you want to do it. List three reasons you want to make your change. (Warning: Obsessing over how you *look* is *always* the *wrong* answer!)

1.
2.
3.

Unscheduled surprises welcome.

monday

tuesday

wednesday

thursday

Thirty days has September, April, June, and . . . oh, whatever.
All I know is a school week has five **LONG** days!

friday

sat./sun.

month _____

monday

tuesday

wednesday

thursday

friday

sat./sun.

Status check! How are you doing on your habit breaking and making? Circle the appropriate number below. Five means "Great!" One means "I don't want to discuss it!"

1.	1	2	3	4	(5)
2.	1	2	3	4	5
3.	1	2	3	4	5

Never put off till **tomorrow** something you can get your little brother to do **today**.

monday

tuesday

wednesday

thursday

friday

Bathing suits are overrated.

sat./sun.

month _____

monday

tuesday

wednesday

thursday

friday

sat./sun.

Monthly wrap-up. Give it up!

It's Monday morning.
Do you know where your homework is?

no more excuses
(or: because i said so!)

It's time to face the music and dance. Is there something you haven't done? Something that makes you just the teensiest bit nervous, like maybe you'd rather pull out your toenails than do whatever it is that's giving you the jitters?

Well, I declare this month National Do It Anyway Month! Talk to that person you've been wanting to talk to, try out for the play, join the rock-climbing club. Whatever!

The Excuse Train stops here. So get off and get on with it! We will be stronger, better, and wiser and WAY excited to have IT over with. Trust me, it will only hurt for a minute.

Power to the pupils!

Is there a dance at your school that you really want to go to? If you do, do you have a date? If you do but you don't (want to go/have a date), what are you planning to do? Rate how you would feel about the possibilities. (Five means "Great idea." One means "And your planet is in *which* galaxy?")

1. I will get the word out that I want to go, then see if I get asked.
1 2 3 4 (5)

2. I will tell a friend (a boy) that I want him to take me.
1 2 3 (4) 5

3. I will go with a group of friends.
1 2 3 4 (5)

4. I will go by myself.
(1) 2 3 4 5

5. I won't go.
(1) 2 3 4 5

Whatever it is – it's not my fault and I definitely didn't do it.

monday

tuesday

wednesday

thursday

friday

Dance-schmance . . . errr . . . unless . . .
I mean, are you asking me?

sat./sun.

month _____

monday

tuesday

wednesday

thursday

friday

sat./sun.

If there's something you've been meaning to do, now's the time to do it. Go back and review all your goals from each month of this year. Then make a final-last-ditch-gonna-get-it-done-here-and-now list!

Final-Last-Ditch-Gonna-Get-It-Done-Here-And-Now List
1. Reading Log
2. Grades
3. Homework
4.
5.

I'll get it done . . . someday.

Report cards do **NOT** tell the whole story.

monday

tuesday

wednesday

thursday

friday

sat./sun.

month _____

monday

tuesday

wednesday

thursday

friday

sat./sun.

You must have some note-worthy notes! Jot away!

I did it!
(Whatever it was.)

free time - finally!

Excuse me, but how cool is it to be organized enough to finally be able to do some of those things you could never get around to before?

Way.

That's how cool.

Personally, I'm going to answer all the questions I'm asking you in the next couple of pages and then I'm going to figure out where they go in my schedule.

Stand back and be amazed, world. We the organized, we the nonchaotic RULE!

Get ready, get set, get to it!

month _____

monday

tuesday

wednesday

thursday

friday

sat./sun.

What are you going to do with your free time? There are books to read and places to go and people to see and letters to write and cool things to make and whatever! It's time to figure out when you can do the stuff you really want to do.

The book I really want to read is: Captain underpants

The place I really want to visit is: The Spa

The person I really want to see is: Halle Iycess

Ladies! Start your list making!

A girl could get used to this.

month _____

monday

tuesday

wednesday

thursday

friday

sat./sun.

The person I really want to write to is: Jamacell

The person I really want to call is: Halle   Iycess

The art project I really want to create is: None

The brand-new thing I really want to learn is: None

The food I really want to learn how to make is: None

The goal I really want to reach is: None

Dear Diary,
Today I woke up.

monday

tuesday

wednesday

thursday

friday

sat./sun.

Reading a book a week is not the **worst** idea you've ever had.

month _____

monday

tuesday

wednesday

thursday

friday

sat./sun.

This month is outta here! Talk about it!

Was I dreaming or is it
the end of another month?

cash flow management

How's the old cash flow these days? I know—it's a sensitive subject, especially if the powers-that-be won't give you a driver's license or a job. But hey, we are Organizational Superheroes. We've faced worse (the chaos of our preplanner days) and survived.

Personally, I'm picking up the odd dollar with a little baby-sitting around the neighborhood. It's a pretty good gig since all the kids I'm wrangling just want to run around outside. Once I secure the perfect lawn chair position, all I have to do is make sure they don't terrorize the neighborhood cats. Occasionally, I'm used as a human jungle gym, which, I'll admit, doesn't do much for my hair—but, all in all, I've got some cash in my pocket to see the movies I want to see or to take those little day trips to the amusement park.

I mean, hello?! How cool is that?

Okay. Snap to! It's time to increase the cash flow! Can you think of five things you could do that might fatten up your piggy bank?! I'll get you started:

1. Baby-sit
2. Mow lawns
3. Rake Decks
4. Sweep Kitchens
5. Read a book to babies

Everybody's got a different idea about the best way to save money – put it in the bank, give it to your parents to hold, or invest in really valuable trading cards . . . err, whatever. But the bottom line, in my very humble-Lizzie-opinion, is this: The Way to Save Money Is Not to Spend It! Duh.

What's your plan?

Brother, can you spare a **dime?**

monday
tuesday
wednesday
thursday
friday
sat./sun.

Who needs money – especially when you've got a credit card?

month _____

monday

tuesday

wednesday

thursday

friday

sat./sun.

Now that you're a working person, you need to remember to take a little time for yourself. But beware. Relaxation is an art many adults have forgotten. As with any art form, it demands focus, commitment, and everyday practice! So don't be intimidated. When you're hanging upside down off the couch, blowing bubble-gum bubbles and staring at a game show in a foreign language, do not let your mom tell you you're wasting time. Inform her (politely) that you are firmly committed to the deep art of relaxation. (But don't try this too many times . . . it might get a little old.)

Shouldn't I be paid for my **natural charm?**

monday

tuesday

wednesday

thursday

friday

Shopping is just a **darn** good idea.

sat./sun.

month _____

monday

tuesday

wednesday

thursday

friday

sat./sun.

Another month flies by! What did you do?

_____
_____
_____
_____
_____
_____
_____
_____
_____
_____
_____
_____
_____
_____
_____
_____
_____

I am so **not** employed.

relaxation is an important organizational tool

Personally, I have a regular appointment with the grass in my yard. I lie down on it and stare at the sky until I have some profound new idea about how I can get more organized. Sometimes it becomes necessary to close my eyes in order to focus.

I'm not suggesting that sitting (or lying) and staring is the wisest way to spend all your time. But I do think a little bit of time dedicated to sitting and staring has great and lasting benefits. So, lie back, take a big old breath— blink a long, slow blink – and relax!

month _____

monday

tuesday

wednesday

thursday

friday

sat./sun.

The bottom line about TIME OFF . . . You can't work all the time no matter how mind-crushing reality might be. I suggest you schedule the following things into your calendar:

Monthly: See two movies (minimum), brave the unknown and go somewhere you've never been (even if it's just the next block), go to a dance, or if you can't, go to a party, or if you can't, go roller-skating. Or if you can't, go to the mall (see weekly schedule).

Weekly: Go to the mall, read a book (unassigned!), make a surprise for someone.

Daily: Laugh at least three times with friends (preferably not at someone else's expense).

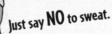

Just say **NO** to sweat.

monday

tuesday

wednesday

You may call it **sleep.** I call it equal time for my eyelids.

thursday

friday

sat./sun.

month _____

monday

tuesday

wednesday

thursday

friday

sat./sun.

And not that you asked, but . . . reading is one of the coolest ways to take time off, so here are the books I think are MUST READS – depending on your mood:
1. FUNNY: *Super Fudge*
2. TOUCHING: *Because of Winn Dixie*
3. FANTASTICAL: *The Giver*
4. ROMANTIC: *Tuck Everlasting*
5. SERIOUS: *Out of the Dust*

And here are a few movies – including some old ones you might not have heard of – that will help you smile through the pain and agony of obtaining a formal education:
1. *Princess Diaries*
2. *Max Keeble's Big Move*
3. *My Bodyguard*
4. *The Karate Kid*
5. *Harry Potter and the Sorcerer's Stone*

Excuse me while I do my toenail exercises.

monday

tuesday

wednesday

thursday

friday

Can you make a living as
a professional **relaxer**?

sat./sun.

month _____

monday

tuesday

wednesday

thursday

friday

sat./sun.

We bid *adieu* – how'd you do? Make it good!

Organizational Superheroes Unite
(in alphabetical order, please)!

the lowdown on friends, neighbors, and countrymen (and women)

We're talkin' the basic 411

---

name: _Alexis_

phone: _____

address: _____

cell phone: _____

e-mail: _Alexis @ yahoo. com_

birthday: _____

---

name: _____

phone: _____

address: _____

cell phone: _____

e-mail: _____

birthday: _____

---

name: _____

phone: _____

address: _____

cell phone: _____

e-mail: _____

birthday: _____

name: _____ phone: _____

address: _____ cell phone: _____

e-mail: _____ birthday: _____

name: _____ phone: _____

address: _____ cell phone: _____

e-mail: _____ birthday: _____

name: _____ phone: _____

address: _____ cell phone: _____

e-mail: _____ birthday: _____

name: _____ phone: _____

address: _____ cell phone: _____

e-mail: _____ birthday: _____

name: _____   phone: _____

address: _____   cell phone: _____

e-mail: _____   birthday: _____

name: _____   phone: _____

address: _____   cell phone: _____

e-mail: _____   birthday: _____

name: _____   phone: _____

address: _____   cell phone: _____

e-mail: _____   birthday: _____

name: _____   phone: _____

address: _____   cell phone: _____

e-mail: _____   birthday: _____

holidays

the best part of any month

January

_____

_____

_____

February

_____

_____

_____

March

_____

_____

_____

April

_____

_____

_____

May

_____

_____

_____

June

_____

_____

_____

July

_____
_____
_____

August

_____
_____
_____

September

_____
_____
_____

October

_____
_____
_____

November

_____
_____
_____

December

_____
_____
_____

days to remember

Birthdays, anniversaries, vacation days, and other dates that you must, must remember this year:

spread the word
(but don't blame me if you get caught)

Hel-l-l-l-lo?
I thought I told you
this already. . . .

Please Deliver To:

_____

Mind your own business
(in the nicest possible
way) and pass this to

_____.

Thank you.

This note contains:

[ ] personal information

[ ] school business

[ ] VERY personal information

[ ] answers to the test
you're taking right now

[ ] nothing of any importance –
just wanted to say hi

Dear Teacher,

This note was passed on October 4, 1943. The
person you just took it from is nothing less than
a very accomplished archaeologist, as that person
just discovered a 60-year-old artifact. Please do
not mistakenly punish the archaeological prodigy
by thinking this is actually a note that she passed.
That would be a sad miscarriage of justice.
Rather, give that student an A for the day and
order a pizza.

Signed,
Note-Passing Student of 1943

Hel-l-l-l-lo?
I thought I told you
this already. . . .

Please Deliver To:

_____

Mind your own business
(in the nicest possible
way) and pass this to

_____.

Thank you.

This note contains:

[ ] personal information

[ ] school business

[ ] VERY personal information

[ ] answers to the test
you're taking right now

[ ] nothing of any importance —
just wanted to say hi

Dear Teacher,

This note was passed on October 4, 1943. The
person you just took it from is nothing less than
a very accomplished archaeologist, as that person
just discovered a 60-year-old artifact. Please do
not mistakenly punish the archaeological prodigy
by thinking this is actually a note that she passed.
That would be a sad miscarriage of justice.
Rather, give that student an A for the day and
order a pizza.

Signed,
Note-Passing Student of 1943

the general state
of the union . . .

That is to say, this is your free time, your recess, your study period.
Go wild, go nuts – talk about it! (Whatever IT is.)

_____
_____
_____
_____
_____
_____
_____
_____
_____
_____
_____
_____
_____
_____
_____
_____
_____
_____
_____
_____